HAL•LEONARD
INSTRUMENTAL
PLAY-ALONG

AUDIO
ACCESS
INCLUDED

PLAYBACK+
Speed • Pitch • Balance • Loop

FLUTE

Gospel Hymns

To access audio visit:
www.halleonard.com/mylibrary

Enter Code
7101-6462-4680-2738

ISBN 978-1-4950-7379-3

HAL•LEONARD®
7777 W. BLUEMOUND RD. P.O. BOX 13819 MILWAUKEE, WI 53213

In Australia Contact:
Hal Leonard Australia Pty. Ltd.
4 Lentara Court
Cheltenham, Victoria, 3192 Australia
Email: ausadmin@halleonard.com.au

Visit Hal Leonard Online at
www.halleonard.com

AMAZING GRACE

FLUTE

Words by JOHN NEWTON
Traditional American Melody

rit.

BLESSED ASSURANCE

Lyrics by FANNY J. CROSBY
Music by PHOEBE PALMER KNAPP

Flute

Moderately, with feeling

DOWN BY THE RIVERSIDE

FLUTE

African American Spiritual

HE'S GOT THE WHOLE WORLD IN HIS HANDS

FLUTE

Traditional Spiritual

HIS EYE IS ON THE SPARROW

FLUTE

Words by CIVILLA D. MARTIN
Music by CHARLES H. GABRIEL

IN THE GARDEN

FLUTE

Words and Music by
C. AUSTIN MILES

LEANING ON THE EVERLASTING ARMS

FLUTE

Words by ELISHA A. HOFFMAN
Music by ANTHONY J. SHOWALTER

THE OLD RUGGED CROSS

FLUTE

Words and Music by
REV. GEORGE BENNARD

PRECIOUS MEMORIES

FLUTE

Words and Music by
J.B.F. WRIGHT

SHALL WE GATHER AT THE RIVER?

FLUTE

Words and Music by
ROBERT LOWRY

SWEET BY AND BY

FLUTE

Words by SANFORD FILLMORE BENNETT
Music by JOSEPH P. WEBSTER

THERE IS POWER IN THE BLOOD

FLUTE

Words and Music by
LEWIS E. JONES

WAYFARING STRANGER

FLUTE

Southern American Folk Hymn

WHEN WE ALL GET TO HEAVEN

Flute

Words by ELIZA E. HEWITT
Music by EMILY D. WILSON

WHISPERING HOPE

FLUTE

Words and Music by
ALICE HAWTHORNE